100 Irish Tunes for B Flat Flute

This book is designed as a resource to introduce the student to the B Flat Flute which isn't as popular as other flutes such as concert flutes or wooden, keyless folk flutes in the rest of the world, but in Ireland and some parts of the UK this instrument plays a big part in celebrating their cultural identity through traditional music and colourful marching bands. The book includes 100 tunes from Ireland or associated with Ireland to help the student to improve their repertoire.

Written and compiled by

Stuart Boyd

Stuart Boyd

22 Melrose , Stafford

UK, St179FY

ISBN-978-1-4478-1294-4

Printed by Lulu.com

To assist students with understanding the abc notation, all tunes will be available on Youtube at the following address,

www.youtube.com/user/Accordionstu

Looking after your flute

There are a few different types of flutes on the market made from a variety of materials and cleaning and caring for the type of flute you have will depend on which material it is made from.

Miller Wicks N.I Flutes

www.millerwicks.co.uk

Wooden Flutes

Miller Wicks, Millyard Molem, Peter Worrell, Mullan, Mull Wilks, Crown AZ's, Ruddal and Carte and Potters are the main types of wooden flutes that I have come across over the past 25 years.

They are all made out of African Blackwood or similar Blackwood's and although it has a good level of moisture resistance, being wood it will dry out in warmer climates and at higher ambient temperatures. African Blackwood or Mpingo is harvested at an unsustainable rate and current stock levels are in decline but demand is greater than ever. This will unfortunately reflect on the price of flutes in the future unless a different wood is used such as cocobolo or rosewood.

A wooden flute will take a few months of regular playing to settle properly. The process is called 'Blown in' and it just means that the pads will settle to make a good seal over the holes and the cork will settle to ensure a good seal etc.

It is advisable to clean your wooden flute with oil on a regular basis. I clean my flute once a week and use a small amount of oil soaked onto a cotton ball. Just rub the oil over the body flute and between the keys. Oil the head joint too and rub the oil into the wood for a good five minutes.

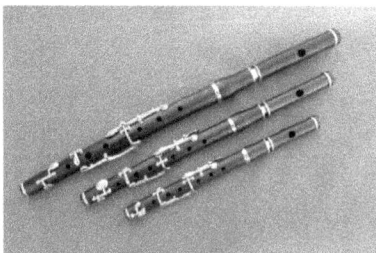

Left: The Family of Millyard Molem wooden flutes.

I then take the flute in a cloth rag or duster and use a simple pull through with a small screw tied on one end of a piece of cord and a small strip of cloth soaked in oil, tied to the other end.

Remove the head joint from the body of the flute so that the flute is in two halves, then drop the screw down the inside of the body and let it drop out of the bottom. Then gently pull the screw and the cord and the oil soaked strip of cloth will be dragged down the barrel, cleaning the inside of any spit residue and it will soak into the wood making it water resistant for a short period of time.

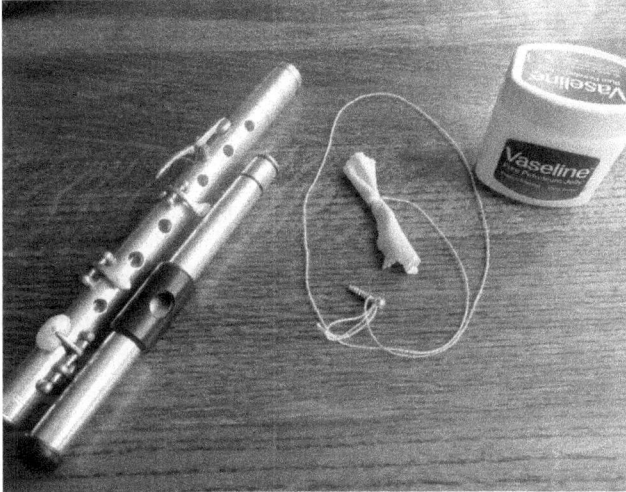

Oil is fine on wood but the leather pads don't like oil at all, so I fold a small piece of newspaper the size of a postage stamp in half and tuck it underneath the key pads to stop any oil settling on the pads.

The inside of the head joint is cleaned by using a thin piece of wood or pencil and ram rodding a small cotton ball with a little oil down to just under the embouchure hole and then pulling it back and forth a few times to clean and coat the inside of the head joint.

Care needs to be taken not to disturb the cork otherwise you may send your instrument off key and you won't sound like the rest of the flutes in the band. An experienced band captain will be able to tune this back relatively quickly and all flutes should be checked and tuned before a parade to ensure there are no surprises.

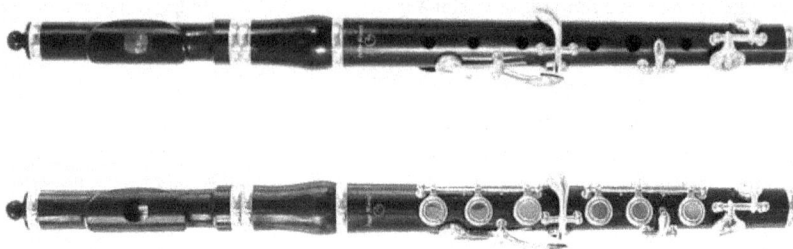

Two flutes from Peter Worrell

The cork should be left alone and never allow the head to be knowingly immersed in water. Water will put stresses on the cork and pads and will affect the sound of the flute.

When not playing the flute it should be stored away from heat or damp, never leave one on a radiator or window sill or even on the back shelf of the car as they will dry out quicker than you think and if the instrument gets warped then its no use to you anymore.

If you do notice any cracks in your flute, don't try to repair them yourself. There are some very skilled instrument makers amongst our community and all those mentioned earlier will be able to repair your flute professionally. A bad repair can make the crack worse.

If you don't already have a flute case for storage, visit some of the websites listed in the back of the book and enquire whether they have any for sale. Protecting your flute will keep it in good order for many years and if you do decide to part with it for a different type, you will get a fairer price if it's been well looked after.

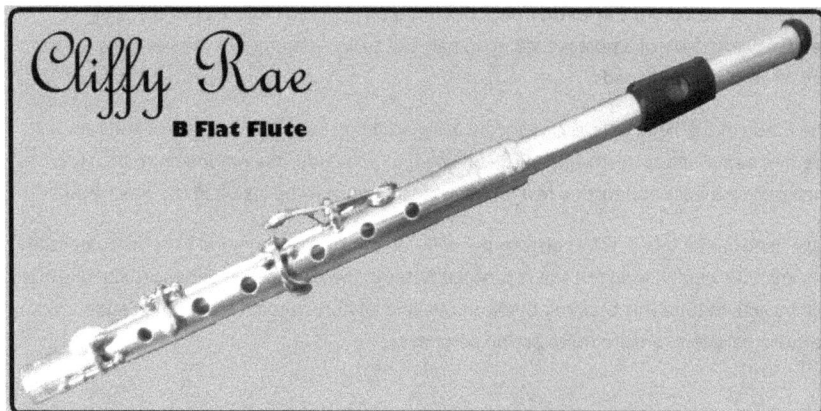

Metal Flutes

The only one that I am aware of at the moment is the Cliffy Rae flute. There have been a few models from Clifford Rae over the years and his latest model is a fine instrument.

Being metal it is hard wearing and doesn't require much maintenance except to clean the inside with a cotton ball after playing. Unlike a wooden flute it isn't porous and doesn't require oiling or polish. The metal flutes are anodised and are totally waterproof. The head joint is one piece and is attached to the flute by a tenon with two or three rubber O-rings which help make a perfect air seal.

It is important to remove the head joint as soon as you get your flute and apply a little amount of Vaseline or silicone grease to the o rings to enable the head joint to be removed easily each time.

The cork in the Cliffy Rae is made of hard plastic and is less likely to suffer from the same issues as a proper cork but you should still take care when cleaning. The embouchure is enclosed in a plastic raised lip plate which is handy especially in cold weather.

I have heard tales from band members that metal flutes tend to seize up in very cold weather and I could only advise that you keep the instrument close to your flesh and keep it warm before playing it on a cold day parade.

As the instrument is impervious to most other issues that the wooden flute suffers from, I feel that these flutes will be with us for a long time.

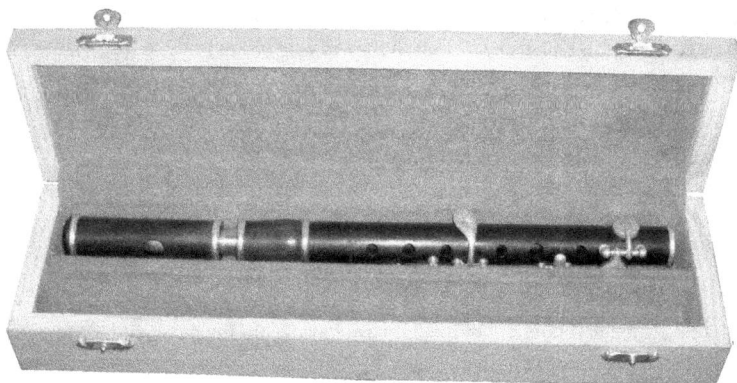

Plastic Flutes

It sounds horrible but flutes made out of Ebonite, a type of vulcanised hard rubber or Bakelite, the world's first synthetic plastic have been around since the 1930's with varying successes.

Rudall & Rose made a few decent models of B Flat and F Flutes in Bakelite and today there are Miller Browne's, Browne Wicks, Crossett's, Ferris, Drum sounds etc. Many of these are made in factories in India or China and with few exceptions they lack the quality and consistency of the makers of wooden and metal flutes.

In my opinion the best of these types on the market is the well-established Miller Browne flute. Not only because it has been around for over 30 years but spares can be purchased inexpensively and they are readily available.

Made from Ebonite it is water resistant inside and out and needs little maintenance except to be cleaned with a little oil on the inside and light brush against the base of the keys to get rid of dead skin and spray with a little lukewarm soapy water on the outside and cleaned with a cotton ball.

The head joint should be treated as the wooden head joint and the pull thru can be used on the Miller Browne too.

Again if you can buy a simple case for your flute, they can be bought second hand on ebay at the moment for a tenner alternatively use a long card tube used to send posters in the mail, they can be bought from the stationer for a couple of quid at the maximum.

Learning to play the Flute

I would recommend asking a flute player to play your flute before you even try, this is to make sure that it doesn't have any defects. If they can play all the notes easily then you won't be able to make excuses and blame the flute later.

It isn't easy to blow the flute otherwise everyone would be playing them, it takes patience and control and a lot of practice to be able to get the notes sounding as they should do and if you follow the next few steps you will be on the right path to mastering the blowing technique.

Step1 – Remove the head joint.

It is easier to get the first note out of the flute by blowing into the head joint alone. Place the head joint between both hands and place the embouchure hole directly under the middle of your bottom lip.

There is a recess between most peoples lip and chin and the contour of the head joint fits nicely into this recess. You shouldn't have to press it hard against your flesh and relax your grip so that you can concentrate on your tongue.

Step 2 – Dry Spit

Once you are ready, inhale enough air to fill your lungs about ¾ full and imagine there is a small piece of tobacco in the middle and at the edge of your bottom lip, You are going to try to blow this piece of tobacco off your lip and down into the embouchure hole. The secret however is not to spit a gobfull of saliva all over the place when doing it.

Practice doing this in front of a mirror and watch as when you exhale the air a little hole opens between your lips, this should be a very small hole and shouldn't sound too breathy.

Try dry spitting for a split second and listen out for a noise that sounds like a flute. Keep doing this until you can hear the noise and you may need to twist the head joint slightly to get the right sound. Once you have mastered this move on.

Step 3 – Replace the body of the flute

At first don't try covering any holes, just hold the flute as before with one hand on either end as if you were about to eat a corn on the cob and once you have lined the head joint up again, try dry spitting into the embouchure hole again.

You might be a little frustrated that it is more difficult than before and this is because the tube that you are trying to fill with air has got longer and it will take a little more effort to be able to reach the note.

Keep practising this until you can do it by picking the flute up and blowing the note first time. The note you are trying to hit is called C sharp (C#).

If you are struggling, remove the head joint and go back to Step1 and keep going until you have got it. This can be achieved within a day or could take some people weeks depending on the muscles in their mouth and breath control.

Step 4 – Hold it properly

Once you have mastered the first note you can have a go at holding the flute properly. The thumb on your left hand should be placed parallel to the top of the first hole and the three fingers on your left hand should be resting beside the first three holes. Your little finger will hover over the G# key.

The thumb of your right hand should rest underneath the 4th hole with the three fingers resting at the side of the next three holes. The little finger should be resting on top of, but not pressing with any force on top of the bottom key (D#)

Lift the flute up and line up the head joint as earlier and try to dry spit c# again. If this is achievable then you could try covering the first hole with your left index finger and you should hear a sound which relates to the note B.

At the back of the book you will see a finger chart for all the notes you will need for most tunes. I would advise starting with low d and working your way across each page until you can play all the notes properly and easily before moving on to learning your first tune.

Learning the first tune

The first tune I learned and most people learn in flute bands is the national anthem. The beauty about learning the B Flat Flute is that most of the traditional tunes we play in the bands are tunes that we know and either whistle or sing the melodies long before we even play them. The tunes are part of our culture and we have the benefit over other musicians in that we know what the tune should sound like and once we have the notes in front of us, we don't need to know how long to hold the note for or whether it should be played this way or that way, we should be able to play it from our own memories.

Playing by ear is a skill and one that amazes other musicians and non-musicians in other parts of the world, but it feels normal to most bandsmen and women in our own culture and that is one of the traits that makes us unique.

There are of course many tunes which are more difficult to learn by ear and be able to recall as easily especially marches and tunes which have multiple parts arranged, these parts can be unrecognisable as being part of the tune when played on their own and it is with the rest of the band that they come to life and don't sound great to whistle to either.

As we have already decided that we know how the tune should sound, we support this by using a simple abc system instead of having to learn how to read music. In hindsight I wish that I had learned to read music a lot earlier in my musical career as the abc system has a limitation but it is still the preferred method of learning simple tunes quickly for most flute bands today.

The system I use in the previous B Flat Fluters Companion is the same one that I use in this book.

All low notes are in lower case, all notes in the middle register are in capitals and all high notes have a ' beside the capital.

'abc' Notation

This primitive method for writing music has been around in many forms for hundreds of years. It is the preferred method for learning tunes quickly by B Flat Fluters in Ireland and across the UK because of it's simplicity and as most tunes that are played have a cultural significance, the fluter will no doubt know most of the tunes from songs they have heard as a child in social gatherings such as Birthday's Weddings and Wakes.

It's easier to play any tune once you have committed the tune to memory and when you understand the basic abc notation, it is even easier. There are other forms of abc notation associated with traditional music sites but the form in this book isn't the same, whereas they use lower case letters for high notes, I use capital letters and for higher notes I use the 'symbol after each note.

There are 33 notes on the B Flat Flute and they are split up into three registers or octaves.

The lowest register starts on low d and runs up to middle D Then the second runs up to high D' and the third is a half register as it only runs up to high A'.

1st Resister, low d, low d#, low e, low f, low f#, low g, low g#, low a, low a#, low b, low c, low c#, middle D

2nd Register, Mid D, Mid D#, Mid E, Mid F, Mid F#, Mid G, Mid G#, Mid A, Mid A#, Mid B, Mid C, Mid, C#, High D'

3rd Register, HighD', HighD#', HighE', HighF', HighF#', High G', HighG#', High A'

Over the next few pages I have illustrated finger charts which correspond with all the notes, try these out once you have mastered the blowing technique.

Low d

low d#

low e

low f

low f#

low g

low g#

low a

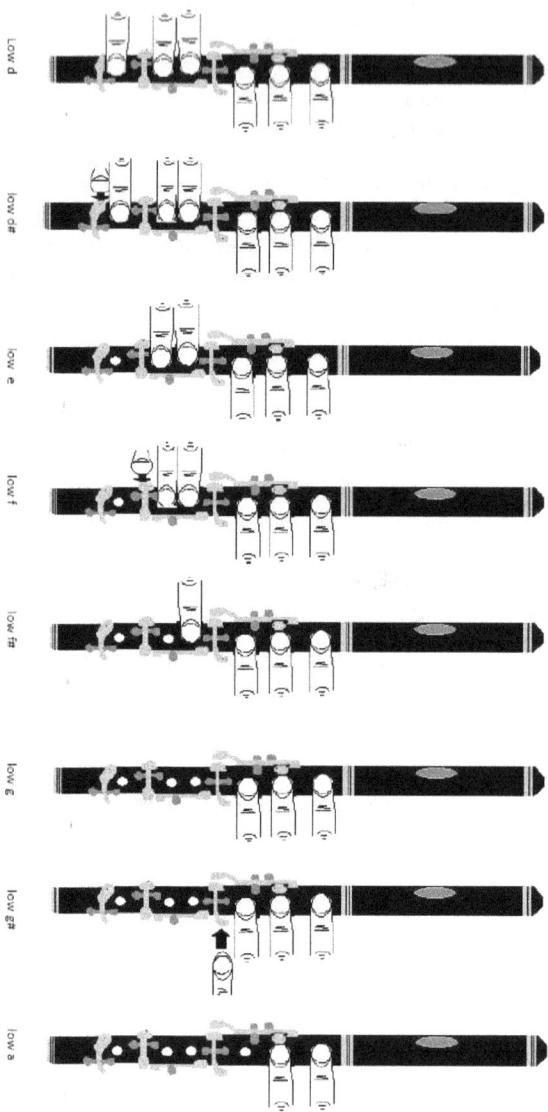

Illustrated by S. Boyd www.stuartboyd.co.uk

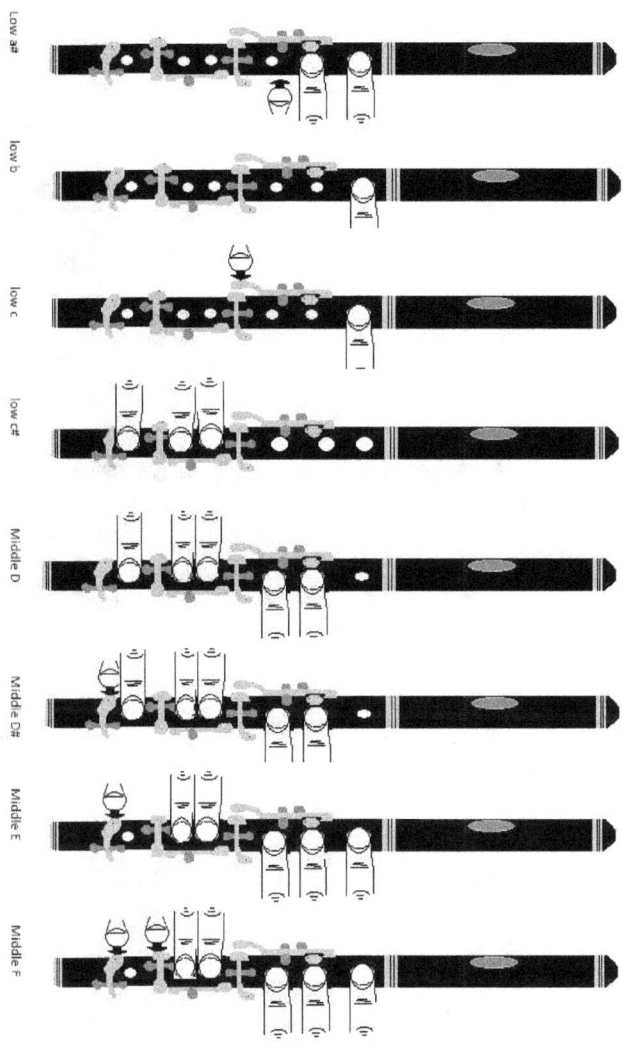

Low a#

low b

low c

low c#

Middle D

Middle D#

Middle E

Middle F

Middle F#

Middle G

Middle G#

Middle A

Middle A#

Middle B

Middle C

Middle C#

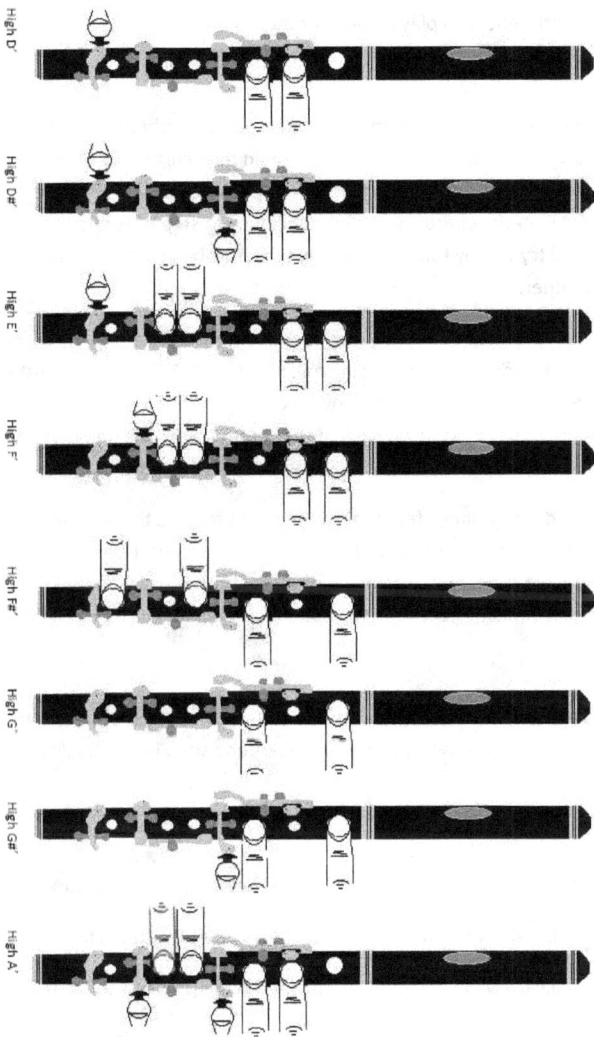

High D'
High D#'
High E'
High F'
High F#'
High G'
High G#'
High A'

Practice, Practice, Practice.

Once you have learned your first tune, practice the hell out of it, play it alongside other fluters too as it is different than playing on your own in the house.

I would recommend practising between 20 -30 mins per day, otherwise your mouth muscles get slack and you won't be able to reach and maintain those high notes for any length of time. Once you get into the flow, you will be learning a tune a day easily. The only thing that restricts most Fluter's repertoire is their reluctance to step outside of their own little political sphere and try to play tunes which may presently be associated with one community or another.

I am constantly searching for different tunes to keep my interest and some of them are included in this book, influences from Italian folk music, Irish Rebel and Loyalist tunes, Chinese folk tunes and Welsh folk tunes, I love them all and the more of us playing and mastering them the better chance we have of these tunes surviving and more importantly, the better chance the B Flat Flute has of surviving through this century.

With marching bands in decline, I fear that we need to promote this instrument more so now than we ever have. Fifes and flutes have been very much part of Irish folk music for over 400 years and we should be encouraging todays youth through societies and musical organisations and any means necessary to ensure that it maintains a place in Irish culture.

I have a series of tutorials on Youtube which have helped hundreds of people to learn how to play the B Flat Flute and below are a list of makers and suppliers of quality instruments mentioned earlier in the book.

Millerwicks Flutes N.I	www.millerwicks.co.uk
Miller Browne Flutes	www.victor-stewart.com
Millyard Molem Flutes	www.millyard-molem.com
Cliffy Rae Flutes	www.esseymusical.co.uk
Peter Worrell Flutes	www.peterworrell.co.uk

Tunes Index

My Dungannon Sweetheart

def#AD F#F# c#EDDD F# AAGGG

E#c#ac#EA C#E AAF#G Ec# ABC#D F#baf#e

F#F# D BAA BAF# BAF# BAGGG

GF#AGEC# AC#E A F#GED ABC#D F# bafe

The Inisheer

D B ABD' B ABD' E BAB D

BAG B ABD' B ABD' G BAGF#G/DED

GBD'E' F#'E'D'B ABD' E'F#'E'D'BD'E'

BD'EF#'E'D'B ABD' G BAGF#G

GBD'E'F#'E'D'B ABD' G'F#'E'D'BD'E'

BD'EF#'E'D'B ABD' G BAGF#G

Eileen Oge

E F# G ABCBAGF#E D EF# GABAGF#ED

E F#G ABCBAG E GABCB ABA GAG F#GF# EF# EE DE

E'E'E' E'D'BGAB BB F#F#F#F#F# AA EEEEE BCB

E'E'G' E'D'BGAB GABCB ABA GAG F#GF# EF#EEDE

The Irish Washerwoman

DCB GG d GG BGBD CB

CAA F# AA CACE

DCB GG d GG BG BD

BCBCA DC B GGG

BD GF#G G B D GF#G BAG

F#E F# f# AD F#EF# AGF#E GG

DGG C# GGb

bcbca Dcbggg

Brian Boru's March

BAG EEE BAG EEE

AGF# DDD AGF# DDD

BAG EEE BAGEEE

b EGABAB GEEE

B EGAB AB AB GE

DEF#A F# AF#A F#E

bEG BAB AB CD'E'

BC BAB GEE

The Kesh Jig

DEDDEF#E F#EEF# A BAA D'AA BAF#A F#E

DEDD EF#EF#EEF# AB AA D' AF#EDc#D

F#E#F# AF#A BD' BAF#E

F#EF# AF#D EF#EE DE

F#E#F# AF#A BD' BAF#E

D'C#D'E'D'EF#' D'C#D'

Paddy's Green Shamrock Shore

D ABC A DA F#GF# D c bcD ED

D' BAGA BCD' CBA D' C BAG DEc

D' BAGA BCD' CBA D' C BAG DEc

D ABC A DA F#GF# D c bcD ED

Fields of Athenrye

DD DGAB BC CCD' B CBGA BCD' E'D' BC D'CBA

BCD'E'D' BC D'C BAGA BA DD AA ABCB AGF#G

D' E' D' G DGAB BAG DG A B BCD' A

D'D'D' BC D'CB AGA BA D AA BCB AGFG

Wild Colonial Boy

D'E'D' GBD' D'E' CA GF# D BAG

D'D' G'G' G'F#'E' A BCD' F#' E' D'

D'D' G'G' G'F#'E' A BCD' F#' E 'D'

D'E'D' GBD' D'E' CA GF# D BAG

Crossmaglen

D D E D D G A B B C B C B G A B

D D E D D G A B B C D' C B G B A

D'C B C B A G C D' C D' C B B C B A G A

D' C B C B A G C D' C D' C B B A G A G F# G

The Green Fields of France

DDED G GGEE ca GGF#F#GABAGcED

DDED G GGEE ca GG F#F# GAB AGG AG

BCD'D'D'D' CBAABC DAABC BAGABA

BCD'D'D'D' CBAAGE D AABCB AGGAG

BBA BAAA ABC D'C BG BA BAA ABCD'CA

ABC CCCD' CBB BAG ABC D' C AGF#G

King of the Fairies

b EDE F#GF#G ABB GF#GA B

EEF#G EF#GF#ED b

EDE F#GF#G ABAG BD' CB EGF#EDE

BCD'E'D'BD'E'F#'G'A'G'F#'E'

F#'E' BBC#D'BC#D'C# BA F#

BABC#DC#D' E'F#'E'D' F#' A'

G'F#' B D'C#BAB

Lord of the Dance

G CC D'E'D'E'F'G'G'E' D'D'D' D'E'F'E'D'CB

GCC D'E'D'E'I'G'G'E' D'D'DF'E'D'CE'C

G'E' D'E'F'E'D'C E'E'F'G'F'E'D'D'D'

GCCC D 'E'D'E'F'G' F'E' D'D'D'F'E'D'CE'C

Holy Ground

F#F# AA GE cDED F#AA BC#D' C#

A D'C# BABAF# F#F# AAGEcDD

F#F# AA GE cDED F#AA BC#D' C#

A D'C# BABAF# F#F# AAGEcDD

Belfast Mill

GB D'D'E'D' GABBCB D' BAABA DDEGGAG

GBD'D'E'D' GABBCBD' BAABA DDEGGAG

Black Velvet Band

DD'ED'BC'D CB AGABGF#ED

D' CBAB DEF#G AB BABCF#G AG

Rare Old Times

F#ED F#A D' BA D'E'F#'D' B

D'D' AA F#GA AAA BC#A BA D'E'F#'D' BA

D'E'F#D' B D'D' AAF#G A F#E F#EF#D

Cockles & Muscles

DGGGG B GAAAAC ABAG D' CBBAGA

DGGGG BGAAAAC ABD' CBD' CB GAG

The Patriot Game

D F#A D' BA F#E AAD D'E'D'E'F#'E'D' BAF#AD'

D'E'D'E'F#'E'D' BAF#AD' DF#A D'BA F#E AAD

I'll Tell My Ma

DDGB BC BB BBAA BAGG

DDGB BCBB BBAA BAGG

D'D'D'BCCC ABBBAGAF#D

D'D'D' BCCC D'CBAG AGF# AGG

The Foggy Dew

BD'E'D'BE'D'BABD EF#G BAGE EDE

BD'E'D' BE'D' BABD EF#G BAG EEDE

GF#G BD' BAAGAB GAB G'F#'E'D'BD'E'

BD'E'D' BE'D' BABD EF#G BAG EEDE

Hot Asphalt

GF#E#F#GF#EDbDGABAGA

BCD'E'D'BAGE BEDDDDEF#

GF#E#F#GF#EDbDGABAGA

BCD'E'D'BAGE BF#EF#EDE

BD'D'D'D'E'D'BGBD'BGBD'

BCD'E'D'BAG EE DDDDEF#

GF#E#F#GF#EDbDGABAGA

BCD'E'D'BAGE BF#EF#EDE

Cooleys Reel

E BBAB EBBCB ABD'BAGF#ED A D BD A D F#ED AD BAGF#E
BBAB EBBCBABD'E'F#'G' A' F#'E'C# D' BA F#D F# AF#E

G'F#'E' BBAB E'B G'F#'E' BBAB G'E'D' BA F#AD AF# BA
F#AD'E'F#'G' E' BBABE'B G'F#'E' BBAB D'E'F#'G' A' F#'E' C#D'
BAF#DF#AF#E

Lannigan's Ball

EE GABABC#D' DDF#GA BAGF#

EE GABABC#D' E' BCBABGEE

EF#G EF#GF#ED EF#G EF# BBB

EF#GEF# GF#ED E'BC ABGEE

Garryowen

D'C# BAGF#ED F#GF#F#

D'C#BAGF#ED EF#EE

D'C#BAGF#ED F#GF#F#

AABC#D' AF#EF#EE

F#GAF#AF#AF#A D'C#BGBGBGB

C#D'E'F#'E'D'C# BA AABC#D'AF#EF#ED

When Johnny Comes Marching Home Again

EEAAA BCBC AGEG

EE AAABCBC D'E'CE'

D'E'E'E'DC D'D'D' BCCC BABBB

CD'E'D'CB AEAAAGA

Rally Round the Flag

GABBBAG EF#GGGF#E

DDcb DGAB CBA

GABBBAG EF#GGGF#E

DDcbDG BA G

D'D' BCD'E' D'D' BCD' D'D' BCD'E'D'D'D' BGA

GABBBAG EF#GGGF#E Ddcb DG BA G

The Sister's Jig

AF#A D'C#D'E'D'C#D' AF#A D'C#D'E'EE

AF#A D'C#D'E'D'C#D' AF# AA EAA F# DD

AF# AAGF#G BBAF#A D'C#D'E'EE

AF# AAGF#G BBAF#AA E AAF#DD

Blackbird

F#AABAG BBAGF# AAF#EF#D E

F#AABAG BBAG E'D'C#BAD' ABA

F#AABAG BBAGF# AAF#EF#D E

F#AABAG BBAG E'D'C#D'E'D' AD'E'

F#'AF#'A G'B'G' G'E'D'C#D'E'D'C#BA

F#'A F#'AF#'A G'B'G' G'E'D'C#D'E'D'C#BA

F#'AF#'A G'BG' GE'D'C#D'E'D'F#'A G'BG' GE'D'C#D'E'D'

ADF#A DF#A D' GBD'E'DB

ADF#A DF#AGF#EE

ADF#A DF#A D'GBD'E'D B

ADF#AGF#ED c#DED

F#'F#'F#AF# F#'E'E'E'

F#'F#'F#'F#' G'G'G'G G'

F#'F#'F#'A F# F#'E'E'E'

F#'F#'G'F#'G'F#'E'D

The Minstrel Boy

DG ACBAG C D'G'F#'G'E'D' BCD'BAG

DG ACBAG C D'G'F#'G'E'D' BCD'BAG

D'G'F#'G'E'F#'G'F#'E'D' D'E'F#'G'F#'E'D'

DG ACBAG C D'G'F#'G'E'D' BCD'BAG

Tipperary

F#GAA ABC#D'F#' F#'E'D' B D' A

F#G AA ABC#D'F#' C#D'E' BC#D'E'

AA ABC#D' F#' F#'G' BD'E'F#'

D'E'F#'F#'F#'D'E'D' BA D'F#'D' E'D'

Waltzing Matilda

GAB CBA BAGABGEF#G ED GB D'D'D'D'CBA

GAB CBA BAGAB GEF#G ED GBD' CBA AAG

D'D'D'D'B G'G'G'F#'E' D'D'D'E'D'D'D' CBA

GAB CBA BAGABGEF#G ED GBD'CBA AAG

Donnybrook Fair

DGF#GAGA BE'E'D'BA BABAGAB AGEEDE

GF#G AGA BE'E'D'BA BABGABAGF#G

F#'G'F#'E'F#'E'D'E'F#'E'D'BAB E'E'D'BA BE'E'E'

F#'G'F#'E'F#'E'D'E'F#'E'D'BA BABGAB AGF#G

The Blackthorn Stick

D'G'F#'G'E'G'E'D'BG AGE DGG F#G ABG BA

D'G'F#'G'A'G'E'D'BG AGE DGGF#G ABGGG

D'E'D'D'G'D'D'E'D'D'G'D'D' E'D'D' G'F#'G'E'D'BA

D'G'F#'G'A'G'E'D'BGAGED GGF#GAB GGG

Planxty Irwin

AD'C# BC#D' AGF#ED A EF#G A c#DE

AD'C# BC#D' AGF#ED GEF#GA DEC#D

AD'D'D' C#D' E'F#'E'E'C#A F#'D'F#'E' D'C#D'BA

BC#D' C# BC#D' AGF#ED GEF#GA Dec#D

Fanny Poer

DG DG ABCBA GF#ED EF#GA

D'C BAG BCD'E' AA GF#GED GF#G

BCD' BCD'D' BCD' GAGG

CD'ECD'E'E' CD'E' ABAA

D'C BCD'E'F#'G' F#'G'A'D'

CBAG BCD' F#G

Si Bheag Si Mhor

GABBAGGAGEDb DEDEF#G A GAB AG

BE AD G bag BE AD GF#G

GABBAG AGAB D'E'D'B AGAD' BAG EE

F#G Dbg BE AD D'E'D'CBAGA GF#G

Wild Mountain Thyme

GABBAG EG BD'E'E'E'D'BD' BD'E'E'D'BAG GABC BAGEG

GED DEGAG BD'E'E'E'D'BD' BD'E'E'D'BAG

GABC BAGEG GED D EGAG

O'Carolan's Concerto

DEF# GGGG F#ED EcDb DaDg DEF#G

AGF#EDG D' BCD' BABC ABCD' BCD'E'

CBGBD'CBAGGF#ED EGEG CGCG DGDG BGBG cEcE
ABAGF#EF#ED DcbcD babcabcD

bcDE cD G BAGF#G

DEF#G E'D'CBAG D'GF#D'F#ECEDEF#

GAF#ED G GBAGF#EF# D'D'D' ECCC

DBBB AGF#EF# D'D'D' ECCC E'CE'C

D'BD'B AGF#EF# DE Cd BC AG DbD

G DbD caEa caEa bDGF#ED cbabc DEF#G A DG BAGF#G

Danny Boy

a DEF# EF# BAF#EDb DF#GA BAF#DF#E

a DEF# EF# BAF#EDb DDEF# GF#EDED

ABC#D' D'C# BA BAF# D ABC#D' D'C# BAF#E

AAA F#' E'E'D' BD' AF# D DDEF# BAF#E Dbc#D

Lord Inchiquin

DGG ABAAG AGF#ED b DB

BAG AGF#ED cbcDEDcba

D'CBB AGG AGF#ED BDC

BAG AGF#ED G babag

DDEF#G AAGAB GBA

BAGABCD'D'E' CBG BA

BAGABCD'D'E'CBG BA

BCBAAAB GF#GED

D'CB AGGAGF#ED bDC

BAG AGF#ED G babag

Boys of the Old Brigade (1)

D' BCD' BCBAGE CBABCAF#DG

D' BCD' BCBAGE CBABCAF#DG

GF#GABCD'D' BCBAGA

D'CB CD' BCBAGE CBABCAF#DG

The Boston Burglar

DBB CD' BBA AG ABGED

DcEG ED GB BBD'CBA

DBB CD' BBA AGABGED

DcEG ED GB BC A F#EF#G

Cronin's Hornpipe

F#EDEF# AAF#A BD'E'D' BABD'

E'F#'E'D' BAF#DE F#EEDE GF#E

DEF# AAF#A BD'E'D' BABD'

E'F#'E'D' BAF#D F# EDDc#D

D'E'F#'E'D'C#BC#D'E'F#'E'D'C#B

C#D'E'D'C#BABC#D' E'F#'E' D'C#

BABGF#GE D EF# AAF#A BD'E'D'BA

BD'E'F#'E'D'BA F# D F# DDc#D

The Town I loved So Well
F#G A AE'D'C#D' D' BA ABC#D' F# DEF# GF#E
F#GA AE' D'C#D'D' BA ABC#D' F# GE D
A☐ D'D'DE' F#'G'G'F'E'D' E'F#'G' G'G'F#'E'D'C#BA
F#GA A E'D'C#D' D' BA ABC#D' F#GED

She Moved Through the Fair
DEF#G AGF#G AA GEcD ED

ABCD' ABA F#GAGF#GA

BCD'☐ ABA F#G AGF#GA

DEF#G AGF#G AA GEcDED

The Net Hauling Song

F# GAF#D AF#D GAGFF#GE

F#G AF#D AF# D C#BC#D'

D'AF# DD F# A D'C#D'E'

D' C#AAA F# GA EF#G

AD'E'F#'D'E'C# AGEF#G

AF# DDDEF#GF#GE

F# GAF#D AF#D GAGF#GE

Sweeney's Polka
D'E'D' BD'A D'B E'F#'G'E'D'BAGE

D'E'D' BD'AD' BD'E'F#'G'E'D'B AGG

BD'G'E'DB AGABD' E'F#'G'E'DBA

BD'E'F#GE'DB AG E'F#'G'E'DBAGG

Galway Girl

BBAG GABGG GGGBD'E'

BBBB GABGG GABBAGF#G

G'F#'G'E'D' ABCCB GABBBAG ABGG

G'F#'G'E'D' ABCCB GABBBAG ABGG

BCBAG AB BCBAG E'E'E'F#'G'F#'E'D'B

D'E'E'D'D' CBAG B AAA BCBAGG

GABAG AB BCBAG E'E'E'F#'G'F#'E'D'B

D'E'E'D'D' CBAG B AAABC BAGG

Maggie in the wood

GDG ABE'E'F#'G'E'D' BAGABAA

BAGDG ABE'E'F#'G'E'D'BABAGG

GDG ABE'E'F#'G'E'D' BAGABAA

BAGDG ABE'E'F#'G'E'D'BABAGG

G'F#'E'D'E'F#G' E'D'BA GABAA

G'F#'E'D'E'F#G' E'D'BA BAGG

G'F#'E'D'E'F#G' E'D'BA GABAA

BAGDG ABE'E'F#'G'E'D'BABAGG

Soldiers Joy

F#GAF#DF#AF#DF#A D'D'

F#GAF#DF#AF#D F#GEE

F#GAF#DF#AF#DF#AD'D'

D'E'F#'A'F#' D'E'G'E'C#D' D'D'

F#'F#'F#' A'G'F#'E'D'C#D'E'F#'G'E'

F#'D'F#'D'F#' A'G'F#E'D'C#BA D'E'

F#'D'F#'D'F#' A'G'F#'E'D'C#D'E'F#'G'

E'F#'A'F# D'E'G'E'C#D'D'D'

Out on the Ocean

BBAGABD'BA BGEDG ABB AGED

BB AGBD'BA BGED G ABGEG ED

BD'E'E'E'D'B E'G'E'ED'B D'D'D'D'

E'F#'GF'E'D'B AG ABD'E'GE'D'BAGED

G ABG EG

Fisher's Hornpipe

ABC# D' AF# AG BAGF#AF#AG
BAGF#DF#D GEGEF#DF#D E
ABC# D' AF# AG BAGF#AF#AG
BAGF# A D' A F#'E'D'C#D'F#'D'

C#D'E'C#AC#E'C# G
'E'F#' D'AD'F#'D' A'
F#E C#AC#E'C# G'F#'E'D'C# BA
AGABGD GBG D'
BAF#DF#AF#D'
ABD'C#BAGF#ED F#D

Ar Erin

GAB DD EG CAB GAB DDEG BCA
GAB DD EG CAB B A G DD E G A G
BCD' BAG BD' E' G'E'D' BAG ABA
GAB DD EG CAB B A G DD E G A G

Galway Shawl

GGF#ED GGABD' D'D'E'BAG BAGE F#

GGF#ED GGABD' D'D'E'BGG BAF#G

Kathleen Mavourneen

BAG D' BG G'F#'E'D'B BB AG#A E'D'C BCBAG

D BAG D' BG G'G'F#'F#'E'CAAG G'G' D' G BCAG

B G'F#'E'F#'F# 'D#'E'D#'E'CB AG F#E EEE GGG F#

D BAG D' BG G'G'G'G'D' E' G'G' D' BGGF#B AAD' CB

BBACE'D' G' E'D' A CCB

BBACE'D' G ED D'D' G

Fiddlers Green

DGABC BAGAB E DGABCBCD'CBA

ACD'EE'D'C BCD'D' D'CBABC AG GF#GA

D BD' BC A F#AG D'E'CE'D'CBA

ACD'EE'D'C BCD'D' D'CBAB AD'C BABAG

Galway Bay

DG BBBBBB AGGF# D CCCCD' ABCB

DG BBBBB D'CBAE F#GA G# A BC F#BAG

I'll Take you Home again Kathleen

BBC AE'C#D' BB AG# ABAG

DBBC AE'C#D' BA F#'F#'E'D'C#D'

D'E'D'C BC C#D' DF#'ED' ABCB

BB BBB C BB BA ABA BC#D'

DBBC AE'C#D' BB AG# ABAG

Donegal Danny

DB CB AGED DEG AGGED

D D'D'D' CBAG GABCBAGA

BAGGGABCE'D' BD'D' CBAGA

BAGGG ABCD'E'D' E'D'CBAGF#GAB

E'D' CBAGF#G

The Girl I Left Behind Me

G'F#'E'D' B GAGE D GGG ABCD' B

G'F#'E'D' BG AGE GF# A DEF# GG

D'BD'E'F#'G'D'B G B D'E'F#'G' F#'

G'F#'E'D' B GAGE GF# A DEF#G G

Dirty Old town

DGAB AG BGD BD'E' D' BAGB

D'E'D'B AGBGD DGBA AGEE

Carrickfergus

D'D'C#BE EF#G A F#F#GF#ED DEF#G E c#c#DED

D'D'C#BE EF#G A F#F#GF#ED DEF#G E c#c#DED

AAA D' D'E'F#'E'D'E'C#A   AAA D'E'F#' F#'G'F#'E'

D'D'C#BE EF#G A F#F#GF#ED DEF#G E c#c#DED

Come to the Bower

AAD F# DEF#G ABAGED

AAD F# DEF#G ABAGED

AD'C#E'D' AAD'D' ABA

BC#D'C#E'D' F#G ABAGED

AAD F# DEF#G ABAGED

AAD F# DEF#G ABAGED

Raglan Road

GABBB ABD'D'E' D' BG BAGGG

D'E'D'E'F#G' BAG BCD' B G' BA

D'E'D'E'F#G' BAG BCD' B G' BA

GABBB ABD'D'E' D' BG BAGGG

Sam Hall

GAB ABGE DEG ABA GAB ABGE DEG

ABCBCD'E' E'D' BBGA GABABGE DEG ABA

GABABGE DEG

Irish Rover

AF#D F#GA D'E'F#'E'C#D' C# BABAF# GF#E

AF#D F#GA D'E'F#'E'C#D' C# BA C#D'E' D'C#D'

AA D'D'E'F#' D'E'F#'E'C#A AA D'D'E'F#'D'E' C# A GF#E

D F#GA D'E'F#'E'C#D' C# BA C#D'E' D'C#D'

Drowsy Maggie

EBE D'EBE EBE AF#D F# E BED'E BE BABC#D'AF#A

EBE D'EBE EBE AF#D F# E BED'E BE BABC#D'AF#A

D'F#D'C#E'C#D'E'F#'G'A' F#'G'E'

D'F#'D'C# E'C# BABC#D'AF#A

D'F#D'C#E'C#D'E'F#'G'A' F#'G'E'

A' F#'G'E'F#' D'E'C# BABC#D' AF#A

Red is the Rose

DGGAB BAGAGED DGGGG BD'E' D'

D'E'E'D'B BD' CBAGE DDG BD'E'D' BA G

Sally Gardens

D DEF# EDF# AF# BF# AF#DF# AF#ABC#D' BAF#EF# Dbab

D DEF#EDF# AF# B F#AF#DF# AF# ABC#D' BAF#EF#D

AD'D'C#D' ABD' F#'D'E'D'BD' BE'E'D'E' BD'E'F#'D'E'D'BD

AD'D'C#D' ABD'F#'D'E'D'BD AF#ABC#D' BAF#EF#D

Swallowtail Jig

EGEE BEEGEG BAGF# DDADD D'C#D'AGF#

GEE BEE GEGBC#D'C# BAGF#GEDE

ABD'E'F#'E'F#'E'D'B ABD'E'F#'E'D'C#D'

ABD'E'F#'E'F#'E'DC# D'C# BAGF#GEDE

Parting Glass

BAG EE DEGGA GAB BBAGAB EE

BAGEE DEGGA GAB E'D' BAB GEE

D'D'BD'E'D'D'D' BD'E'D' BC BA GAB EE

BAG EE DEGGA GAB E'D BABGEE

Shannon Breeze

AAF#DF#AF#G BGD'GBG

AAF#DF#AF#G BAF#ED

ABD'E'F#'D'F#'G'E' G'F#'E'D'B

ABD'E'F#'D' F#A' F# D'F#'E'D'

Off To California

DEF#GF#G BAGED GBD' G'E'

D'E'F#'G'F#'G'D'E'D' BAG ABAGE

DEF#GF#G BAGED GBD'G'E'

D'E'F#'G'F#'G'D'E'D'BAG AGEF#G

D'E'F#'G'F#'E'F#'G'F#'E'D'E'F#'E'D'E'F#'E'D'B

D'G'F#'G' D'E'D' BAGABAGE

DEF#GF#G BAGED GBD'G'E'

D'E'F#'G'F#'G'D'E'D'BAG AGEF#G

Humours of Glendart

ABA F#AF# DF#EF#DF#A BAF#AF#DF#EDE

ABAF#AF#DF#EDE F#A D'C#BAGF#EDc#D

AD'E'F#'D' BABAAF#A D'E'F#'D' F#'E'D'E'F#'D'

AD'E'F#'D' BABAAB C#D'C# BAGF#EDc#D

Sackow's Jig

F# AA GBGF# A D'F#'E'D'

C#BC#ABC#D' F#'E'D'AG

F# AA GBGF# A D'F#'E'D'

C#BC#ABC#D' F#'E'D'

D'BBF#'BBD'BD'F#'E'D'

C# AAE'AAC#AC#E'D'C#

D'BBF#'BBD'BD'F#'E'D'

C#BC#ABC#D' F#'E'D'

Boys of Bluehill

D' BBAF#AD F#GAB ABC#D'E'

D'E'F#'A'G'F#'E'G'F#'E'D'F#'E'D'B

D' BBAF#AD F#GAB ABC#D'E'

D'E'F#'A'G'F#'E'G'F#'E'D'

F#'G'A'F#'D'F#'A' G'F#'E'F#'G'A'B '

A'G'F#'A'G'F#'E' G'F#'E'D' F#'E'D'B

D' BBAF#AD F#GAB ABC#D'E'

D'E'F#'A'G'F#'E'G'F#'E'D'F#'E'D'B

Down By The Glenside

BAB EF#E DEG ABD'B

ABEF#E DEG ABD' B

AB E'F#'E' EF#G AGF#D

EF#G ABD'B ABEF#E

Nut Brown Maiden

DG F#ED G D DG BCBBA

CBD' BD' D DGAB ABC AG

BCD'E'D' BD' B BCD'E'D' BA

CBD' BD' D DGAB ABC AG

Spancill Hill

BB E B BAF#D EF#AF#E DE

BB E'E'F#'E'D'B C#D' D'D'C#BA

BB E'E'F#'E'D'B C#D' D'D'C#BA

BB E B BAF#D EF#AF#E DE

Harvest Home

AF#D AF#AD AF#AD'E'F#'E'DC#BG E'BF#'BG'BF#'B

E'F#'E'D'C# BABAGF#ED AF#AD AF#AD AF#AD'E'F#'E'D'C#BG
E'D'C#D'F#'E'D'C#D' F#'D'

C#D'E' AABA F#AABA G'AF#'AE'AABA E'AF#'AG'AF#'A
E'F#'E'D'C#BABAGF#ED

AF#AD AF#AD AF#AD'E'F#'E'D'C#BG E'D'C#D'F#'E'D'C#D'
F#'D'

The Merry Ploughboy

BCD'D'D'E'BD'C ABC CCD'CB

CBACF#' E'E'D'A CD'A CBG

BCD'D'D' E'E' BCD'CBA ABC CCD'D'CB

CABCF#' E'E'D' A CD'ACBG

Boulavogue

GGDG BD'G' F#'E'G' E'D' E' B AGA GE

F#GDG BD' G'F#'E'G' E'D'E'BA G AGG

D'D'BD' E'F#'G'F#'E'G' E'D'E'B AGAGE

F#GDG BD'G'F#'E'G' E'D'E'B AG AGG

James Connolly

ADD F#AA AD'F#'E'E'D' ABD' BAF# DEEF#E

AF#DD F#AA AD'F#'E'E'D' ABD' BAF# DEF#ED

The Rising of The Moon

GABBBAB D' BBAABA

D'E'D'G'F#'E'D'B GAGGAG

GABBBABD'D' BBAABA

D'E'D'G'F#E'D'B GAGGAG

Sean South From Garryowen

GABABD GBAG DEGGAG

BCD'D'D'BD'E'E'D' BGE CBA

BCD'D'D' G'F#' E'E'D BG BCD'A

GABABD GBAG DEGGAG

Look At The Coffin

D'D'C#D' BAG G'G'F#'G'E'D'C CCD'E'D'B BBBAGA

D'D'C#D' BAG E'E'E'CD'E'D' D' E'E'E'G'F#' E'D'E'D'

B E'D'E'D''CBA

The Spanish Lady

DDDEF#GGGAB CAB GE DD

DDDEF#GGGAB CAB GE DD

BD'D'D' BAGABCD'D'D' BAGA

BD'D'D' BAGA ABC ABGEDD

DDDEF#GGGAB CAB GE DD

DDDEF#GGGAB CAB GE DD

A Nation Once Again

AABC#D'' D'E'F#'F#'E'D' C# BE'D'C#BC#E'D'

AABC#D'' D'E'F#'F#'E'D' C# BE'D'C#BC#BA

AABC#D'E' AA ABC#D'E'F#'

D'C#BB G'F#'E'D' C# BAF#'E' C#D'

A F#'E'D'C#B BG'F#'E'D'C#

C#BB G'F#'E'D' C# BAF#'E' C#D'

Roddy McCorley

D BABD GBAG DEGGAG

BCD'D'D'BD'E'E'D' BG BCD'A

BCD'D'D'BD'E'E'D' BG BCD'A

D BABD GBAG DEGGAG

Four Green Fields

D'C#BA F#AB GF#A D'C# BA ABBBC#D'C#

A F#'E'F#'D' F#'D' G'F#'F#'E' A F#' E'F#'D' ABBBC#D'C#

D'F#' A' G'A'F#' F#'F#' D' G'F#'F#'E' ABC#D'A

G'F#' E'D' F#'E'F#'D'

Monto

AD'E'F#'E'BBAABB D'E'F#'E'BBAC#D'

AD'E'F#'E' BBB BAAA ABBB AD'E'F#'E' BBB AC#D'

AD'E'F#'E'BBAABB D'E'F#'E'BBAC#D'

Henry Joy

GED EG BD'C BGAB GE DE

GED EG BD'C B GAB GE DE

BCD'D'E'D' BD'C B GEG CD'A

GED EG BD'CB GABG EEE

Free The People

G'F#'G' E'D'B GGA D'D' GG'F#'G'E'D' B GGAAGF#G

GB D'D'D'D'E'D'D' BAGGAG GGEG CBCA

GB D'D'D'D'E'D'D' BAGGAG GGEG CBAGG

E'F#'E'D'B CBAGD'

G'G'F#'G'E'D'B GGA D'D' G'G'F#'G'E'D' B GGAAGF#G

Amhrán na bh Fiann

DEF#Da Dc# bag baba DC#Db c#DE bEDc#

DEF#Da Dc# bagbaba bc#c#c#c# b aa

agf#gef#gaba Dc# bc#baf#e

af#df#a abc#DEF# c#b aDF#EDD

Broad Black Brimmer

GABBB BBAGABGEGD DGGGGGGF#GA

BD'E'D' BGG GABGEGD GABBAGAAGF#G

GCCCD'E'E'E' E'D'BGBD' GABBBBBAGAB

BD'E'D' BGG GABGEGD GABBAGAAGF#G

D'D'CBBAG GCCCE'D' GABBBBBAGAB

BD'E'D' GAGEEGD ABBAGAGEF#G

GCCE' E'E'D'BGBD' GABBBBBAGAB

D'E'D'D' BGG GABGEGD DEGGGAB E'D BAAG

Star of the County Down

EG AAA GA CCD' CD'E'D'C AGEG

EG AAA GA CCD' CD' E'D'C AAA

E'G' E'E'D' C D'D'D' CD'E'D'C A GEG

CBAAA GA CCD' CD'E'D'C AAA

The Leaving of Liverpool

GAB D'CBAG G'E'D' GAB D' E'D'A

D'CB D'CBAG G'E'D' GABD'CBAGG

F#'G'A'F#'D' G'F#'E'D' GAB D'E'D'CBA

D'CB D'CBAG G'E'D' GAB D'CBAGG

GABABD'CBAG BD'D'E'D'

E'F#'G'F'G'E'D'BAG BAABA

GABABD'CBAG BD'D'E'D'

BGCE'D'CBD'BGAGGAG

E'F#'G'F#'G'E'D'BAG BD'D'E'D'

E'F#'G'F#'G'E'D'BAG BAABA

GABABD'CBAG BD'D'E'D'

BGCE'D'CBD'BGAGGAG

A Bunch O' Thyme

BBGF#A CBG D'D' D'C#D'E'D'A

BCD'D'E'D'GB E'E'E'CAG AGF#

BBGF#A CBG

When You were Sweet Sixteen

AF#D F#A D'F#'E'D'B GGEG C#E' D'C#D'A

AF#D F#A D'F#'E'D'B BBC#E'C#BA

A D'E'F#' AF#'G' E' D'D'